T0162343

Chance Ransom

Books by Kevin Stein

Poetry
Chance Ransom (2000)
Bruised Paradise (1996)
A Circus of Want (1992)

Criticism
Private Poets, Worldly Acts (1996)
James Wright: The Poetry of a Grown Man (1989)

Chance Ransom

Poems by

Kevin Stein

University of Illinois Press

Urbana and Chicago

Library of Congress Cataloging-in-Publication Data
Stein, Kevin, 1954–
Chance ransom : poems / by Kevin Stein.
p.   cm.
ISBN 0-252-02598-9 (alk. paper) —
ISBN 0-252-06862-9 (pbk. : alk. paper)
I. Title.
PS3569.T3714C46   2000
811'.54—dc21   99-051006

1 2 3 4 5 C P 5 4 3 2

Acknowledgments

Several poems in this manuscript have appeared previously. Grateful acknowledgment is made to the following magazines: *Another Chicago Magazine:* "While I Burned the August Garden"; *Black Warrior Review:* "Sales"; *Boulevard:* "After Camelot," "In the Kingdom of Perpetual Repair," and "Lyric for the Coroner's Heart"; *Clackamas Literary Review:* "Juliet Prowse and the Cast of *Can-Can* Dance for Nikita Khrushchev, Hollywood, 1959," "Politics of Mop and Sponge," and "Yesterday"; *Colorado Review:* "Upon Hearing Bob Marley Say '. . . Life Is Worth Much More than Gold,' the Trinity Graces My Bug-Spotted Windshield"; *Crab Orchard Review:* "Little Puddles, Spring Buckets, the Earth Awash" and "To the Bookstore Manager Who Stuffs Each Purchase with a *How to Get a Refund* Bookmark"; *Crazyhorse:* "First Day, Container Corporation of America, June 1972" and "March, Where the Kickapoo Bends"; *The Gettysburg Review:* "Because I Wanted to Write a Happy Poem, I Thought of Harry Caray's Dying"; *Hawaii Review:* "Because You're American"; *Indiana Review:* "Beanstalk" and "Husk"; *The Kenyon Review,* "Confessional"; *The Missouri Review:* "Full Moon at Tree Line, San Juan Range, Colorado" and "What I Hate about Postmodernism"; *North Dakota Quarterly:* "In Thanks of Visitations," "One History," and "Poem Buried in a Time Capsule to Be Unearthed Spring 2097"; *Poetry Northwest:* "Halloween, St. Luke of the Poor Oncology Clinic," "Home Economics," and "Late Valentine, with Daisies"; *The Southern Review:* "John Brown's Face," "Our Armor," "That Other Four Letter F-Word the Gods So Love," and "Tomorrow"; *Tamaqua:* "On Landscapes, or Cutting My Son's Hair at the Kitchen Sink"; *TriQuarterly:* "Fishing Naked" and "Gods of the Second Chance."

"Because You're American" was reprinted in *Real Things: An Anthology of Popular Culture in American Poetry* (Bloomington: Indiana University Press, 1999). "Home Economics" was reprinted in *World's Best Poetry* (Great Neck, N.Y.: Roth Publishing, 1999).

"That Other Four Letter F-Word the Gods So Love" is in memory of William Matthews. "Halloween, St. Luke of the Poor Oncology Clinic" is in memory of Dwight Brill.

I'm thankful for support offered by the Illinois Arts Council and by Bradley University, whose contributions granted me time to write some of these poems. I'm grateful as well to the editors of *Indiana Review* for their 1998 Poetry Prize.

For thoughtful advice and encouragement, I am indebted especially to soul compatriots Keith Ratzlaff, Dean Young, and Clint McCown. Thanks also to Douglas Crowe, Robert Fuller, and Kevin Teeven for the community of friendship. Thanks to Jimmy's for the necessary. Thanks to Bea and Lily. Always and immeasurably, thanks to Deb who bears the cup, and to Kirsten and Joseph for their small persons.

ransom, *tr.v.*, 1. To obtain the release of (a person or property) by paying a certain price. 2. To deliver from sin and its consequences. (Middle English *ransoun,* from Old French *rançon,* from Latin *redemptiō.*)

In memory of Dwight Brill,

for Dean Young,

for Debra Lang Stein

Contents

. . . the forms that are given us: a human face, a hand, the breast of a woman or the body of a man . . . melancholy language of the black trees in the snow. . . . This alone is enough to make us forget the grief of the world, or to give it form. In any case, the will to form carries in itself one part of the salvation for which you are seeking. The way is hard and the goal unattainable, but it is a way.

—Max Beckmann

What's good?
Life's good,
but not fair at all.

—Lou Reed

One

In the Kingdom of Perpetual Repair

Sunday A.M. so early even FM crackles church service
   for shut-ins,
fire and brimstone fricatives torqued around a tongue
   as forked
as the red-one-with-tail's pitchfork, both useful tools
   for snaring souls
like me who've sworn off church pew for workbench,
   never mind my cursing
what I can't get right. The deck's three-legged table,

for instance, its mishmash of mismatched pine
   and close-out cedar
lifts in slight breeze then nosedives like a child's
   Easter kite,
salsa and beer sprawled from its swept wings. This should
   bring despair,
say, that of the preacher surveying his cracked flock—
   styptic pencils
and clip-on ties, clown dot rouge, and pantyhose bound

around muzzy melon bellies, the kiddies thwacked with shiny
   vinyl hymnals
he splurged collection money on—but *should* is not *does,*
   despite flimflam grammar,
and Christ, we love each other less for what we are than for
   what we might become.
I love it when the preacher claims to be the Lord's tool,
   wrench or saw
or claw hammer in the Big Guy's big hands, his vowels

sanding my soul's rusty hinges. Creak creak, a door opens.
    Creak creak
the organ hums a hymn amenable to each measure and rise
    of lives built
from the ground up only to be ground down like those
    fresh dead
the morning sermon mourns: So-Close Joe, loser of 237
    straight harness races,
lungs so scarred he wheezed from paddock to gate

only to foam home last; and lonely Colonel Bohart,
    retired U.S. Army,
who collapsed in bath holding Ike, his old stuffed dog
    with ruler built-in
for reasons only a man who loves equally his dog
    and his tools understands.
To wit: Bohart's homemade mailbox, exact size and girth
    of Ike,
designed to bark when its mouth-lid opens. Good dog.

No, good man, the more elusive creature in this church
    of break
and break anew. Creak creak, the hinges need oil.
    Creak creak,
my heart swings open with praise for losers we are
    and those we're not
by grace of a thousand fancy chances, blessed stretch
    by which we catch
Fate's hammer inches above the anvil of our head,

or failing that, still find among the cartoon stars its
    blow brings forth
our own brief comet, incandescent tale we believe
    is beautiful
because we've somehow made something of nothing.

Only gods do that.
We elide to nothing: ice to mist, fist to dust.
    Praise this then:
that long undoing maps our single perfect act.

Garage Museum

Of what we keep amidst the dross
    tossed out—we need most the polyglot
      and forgettable, say, a history
        of beer coolies' increased thermal capacity

from styrofoam to zippered neoprene,
    of Barbie's breasts deflating
      and waist thickening as the same fate
        besets the mommies who buy her.

Oh sure I've waited in line for the bullet
    that got Lincoln, his doctor's bloodied
      cuffs scissored off, or gaped before
        the Elephant Man's Cretaceous skeleton

Michael Jackson bought for who knows what
    vile Neverland ritual, as daily I knelt before
      St. Theresa's sliver embedded in the altar,
        pondering her parts allotted by rank

and wondering what cost most—
    finger folded in prayer, forehead
      crossed in supplication—aghast
        the Church had cannibalized

as hungrily as those lions in the den,
    and this for gold not dinner.
      I fumbled my Latin and the priest shot
        a stern eye that pierced fear but not contrition.

What had become of St. Kevin?
  What of the original: what saintly acts
    had he done and what had *they* done
      to his clean bones? A scapula for the bishop?

Oh don't give forth that disquisition
  on the commodification of saints.
    Of course. We buy the flag
      with UPC stamped upon its stripes.

Forget those monuments to history!
  Forego all admission!
    Endow your own garage Smithsonian
      and love how we keep what we keep

because we do instead of don't—
  Uncle Bob's corncob Eiffel tower,
    that ancient Lincoln cent,
      a tuft of mountain goat's coat,

the arrowhead that probably isn't,
  even my petrified toad with toes poised
    as if to leap but going nowhere—
      all mystery with no reason

and for that reason sublime.
  When Buzz Aldrin knelt in lunar dust
    to deliver slivers
      of the Wrights' plane some soul

had the good sense to save,
  those brothers—dust themselves—
    flew Kitty Hawk to the moon.
      The landfill's our Great Satan.

By hook of gather, by crook of stay,
   by cloister and clutter,
      by kiss-my-ass to logic and utility—
     we ransom the holy keep.

Lyric for the Coroner's Heart

In black and white, today's obit page
bleeds Max Beckmann's "The Trapeze,"
painting I once coveted for a book's cover
but got instead the flippant clip-art clown
resplendent in purple and Chevy orange.
Beckmann hangs assorted drunks and acrobats
upon a distorted trapezoidal bar
that moves nowhere against the collective
static force of their desire to fly.
At bottom, an upturned palm implores
yours or mine to reach in, grab on,
do something about Beckmann's oil-brushed
"futility of human existence," though
what to make of those improbable ones
who get what they want?—cause enough
to fear the bloom of our desires:
Oh red Camaro with overhead cam,
oh sweet chocolate cheesecake,
oh plush lips of some other's beloved,
we all perform without a net.
What weird logic compelled the lawyer
to witness his gaudy billboard hung,
only to have the hulking bulk of
INJURED? CALL PHIL SULLIVAN
collapse smack on top of him?
Oh dear baby who wails all night,
oh bottle-blonde tresses gone green,
oh climber on Everest with storm on wing,
we pay for what we get as well as what
we don't. Take, for instance, the coroner
campaigning for and winning five terms,

thus skilled with angles of trajectory
and hearts flabby with plaque. Imagine
the stroke-scarred or bludgeoned brains
he cradled in gloved hands: Press here
for the glossy holiday *Victoria's Secret,*
there for little Billy on Santa's lap,
press this spot for mommy with a cop's stun gun
when baby won't stop crying—ZAP, CRACKLE, SMACK,
Batman and the Commissioner on the phone,
"It's murder." And it was,
our sad-eyed coroner making *The Today Show*
to lecture surprisingly silent Bryant
on the intricacies of the first ever
stun-gun baby killing.
Oh tickets to *La Bohème,*
oh big house with big windows that water spot,
oh ladder and low-slung electric wires,
what surges through us curls our toes with delight
and dread. Consider, if you will,
wanting to know how each of us goes,
the particulars of departure stitched shut
but never closed. Consider, then,
the dead coroner's obit: He who buried
the poor in his own shiny Sears suits,
he who bought plot and casket for a boy
no one would claim, lost boy with bruised blue eyes,
boy with hair as brown as burnt corn muffins
baked for impatient reporters hungry for dirt.
Oh here's a shovelful, there's a shovelful,
everywhere coffee and corn muffins, E-I-E-I-Oh
scalpel and clamp, oh vials of formaldehyde,
who autopsies the coroner? In the end,
the report says, his heart gave out.

John Brown's Face

When weird John Brown, driving
   his father's prize cattle to market, alone,
only twelve and no abolitionist,
     chanced upon a slave being beaten

with an iron camp shovel, he renegotiated
   ownership. Shovel still red from the fire,
its thwack and whump. *Chattel* was a word
     so close to cattle he had to look it up.

As one often does reading Wallace Stevens,
   the great embroidered parade
dressed in lace doilies hinting there's a body
     under there, if only as sound takes shape

on the lips, "concupiscent" as fleshed
   as any frozen Baskin Robbins treat.
Out of the mouths of babes, it's said,
     and sure enough my four year old

called the line of blacks "chocolate"
   and us two "vanilla," opting
to swirl both in a cone the August sun
     gave the sidewalk most of.

Ah, gravity's a notion you can depend on,
   like a kid's face in the damp aftermath
of learning how things fall beneath
     a beating sun, beneath a shovel swung

by the roped arm of belief. *Sticks and stones . . .*
    John Brown's face . . . *can break my bones . . .*
not Raymond Massey's saucer-eyed movie freak,
      not John Steuart Curry's mural with bible

and rifle . . . *but words, words will never hurt me*
    as much as Brown's portrait—intent,
recalcitrant a dozen years before his unholy mess,
      eyes so bright you hardly see the hodgepodge

of good gone evil in service of idea
    he's raised his right hand to, his left tacked
to a vague flagged standard I can't make out.
      Whose flag? Whose standard?

One night, before the TV screen flings
    skeins of static, photon remnants of The Big Bang
that never came together to make sun, moon,
      any color of us, my wife and I risked

the living room floor, necking like teenagers
    whose parents dozed as heavily as the kids
we'd bedded down and prayed sleep tight,
      the thought of getting caught half the thrill.

Mouth on mouth, no word was spoken,
    though something was being said
amidst all that cosmic background radiation,
      the heave and toss of this rock through space

we'd almost kissed our way beyond,
    when not-so-right Rev. Matt Hale beamed on,
self-proclaimed *pontifex maximus* of World Church
      of The Creator, declaiming before our flag

the relative merits of white face and black,
    of round eye, slant eye, four-eyed Hun,
of Wops and Japs and scarab-wearing Arabs,
        of drunken Mexicans and the scheming Jew,

all the swarthy, thick-lipped mud races
    he'd have depart our teeming shores.
If not these, who would he leave?
        If not these, who would he love?

All day we'd forked potatoes from the garden,
    the sun's long run slunk south from its
June heights, the angle giving everything
        we unearthed shadow and face—potato eyes,

nose, stout chin—surprised disguise
    of the newly born we all come in in.
In and out. As with belief and doubt,
        as with John Brown's raised right palm,

spot I've raised a blister from spade
    and hammer, from turning things inside out,
outside in. Of all things a blister claims,
        I love most its honest increments of pain,

its rising tide confiding our body
    is slave to the mind. Dirt cleaved from,
and as language does, cleaved to
        mounds of Kennebec, Red Pontiac,

the Idaho Blues. What to make of that?
    Oh, soup or immortality!
Listen, I've framed a wall of two by fours
        sixteen inches on center, I've closed

something in and walled something out.
   This, simple perspective—how idea frees
or enslaves. Not the looking but the seeing
      makes a window of a wall.

Upon Hearing Bob Marley Say ". . . Life Is Worth Much More than Gold," the Trinity Graces My Bug-Spotted Windshield

Jesus with Natty Dread, The Father with Spliff,
Holy Ghost Skanking His Les Paul Guitar—
a vision of ineffable befuddlement
as grand as the driver's idling next to me,
whose mug of coffee steeples her car's roof,
she all elbow and knee rifling her lap,
the seat, the cracked dash in search of it.
When the light greens, her rusted Duster
lurches the curve of University and Main,
away on some meandering stop and go
I'll call "Blessed Be the Father, Blessed the Son,
Blessed the Holy Mug in Equipoise."
Something from *Tuesday Morning after the Museum*
soundtracked by Marley's "Jamming,"
anthem to possibility both cursed and blessed.
Take, for instance, that Marley died at 36,
though doing so, he never suffered his song
Muzaked for snacking museum patrons,
above whom a scale model B-17 hangs fire,
its bomb bay threatening a rack of pouched
condiments and perforated salt the great war
kept free for our citizenry. Doll-sized soldiers
man rudder and guns, their faces painted with
the astonished grace of guys in a fix,
same look my father wore sharing a sleeper
with Bob Vega from LA to NY just to split
the train fare neither had alone. Back to back,
they rode the taut belly of a country at war.

Oh sure they slept like dolls, eyes rolled
back in their shining faces. Sure they never
gave a thought to what lay ahead,
who lay beside them. That's bull.
My father froze his ass on Kodiak, Attu, Adak.
Bob Vega busted his in a Normandy pasture,
B-17 a broken cross. My father came home
to marry the incremental tick and tock,
slow accrual of silent dinners eaten
with eyes shut as if he slow-motioned
the Host to his unworthy tongue.
What he sees with eyes shut I can't say,
nor will he, though I've seen the one he calls
"Victory, or Lone Caribou Snuffling at Corpse,"
taken with his stowaway Brownie camera.
Above a soldier frozen to tundra,
the bull's thick rack scallops a V in pewter sky.

One History

The mouse with a human ear stitched
    to its back, Rabin's bloody copy
of "Song of Peace," that slathered poodle pup
    sleeping in the lion's half-closed jaws—
primer for an alphabet we know by heart,

asking *Next time won't you sing with me?*
    in a voice that, save for its cherubic face,
would shatter anvil, stirrup, and drum,
    mechanism that grants us balance
when the news close-ups Julio Inglesias

singing Spanish to Peorians of hairspray
    and polyester polyester polyester,
Julio whispering at song's end, "I hold my body
    because I goose bump when I sing you,"
then the audible whoosh of pheromones,

light's out, credits rolling, and Leno
    after this important commercial break.
By heart, the saying goes. Who ever thought
    that muscle capable of learning anything?
Else why the unbroken breaking of it,

the learning curve a lifetime long
    and sadly nontransferable. Else why
the ache we bellyache over, the stuff
    of endless Oprah, Montel, Ricki greasy hair.
Now heartburn, there's medicine for that.

A galaxy of commercial grimace and relief:
   the white guy always gray enough
to believe he's survived heart*ache* so *burn*'s a cinch.
   Who's to say the heart's the residence
of pain any more than the eye's our source of joy,

say, the sight of a lovely naked body
   sufficient unto itself, as indeed it can be
but often isn't. There's this thing we have
   with touch, math that postulates 1 + 1 is 3,
this thing with body *and* mind that testifies

opposites attract, convinces us to love
   the not us in others, as if, in truth,
we know who we are, are not, are, are not—
   a picture writhing in and out of itself
like the birthday earthworm puzzle

we can't figure out, and if we do,
   what do we get? Truth?—one history
of how reason's palace coup undid faith
   and turned us out in tattered linen.
No, I like my gods with sword and winged feet

divinely unsure of when to use which,
   the way we humans think we know a thing
until we know it not, know it only
   and blessedly as surprise, as I did,
when cruising Main and thinking mostly

of landscaped June lilies, I swerved
   to the giant truckload *SUNDIAL* sale
at Payless Shoes, that you must know
   offered only pairs of cheap *SANDALS,*
of which I gladly bought two.

Halloween, St. Luke of the Poor Oncology Clinic

To be the joke no one laughs at,
    told with conviction
disproportionate to the task, around you
    a table silent as breath. To be the comic
who realizes, halfway through a Polish gag,
    it's a banquet of Krakow émigrés
the agency dispatched him to entertain.
    To wonder how in hell to get out
of this, as does our dutiful Mary,

nurse bulging the red satin suit—all horns
    and tail—offering devil's food brownies
to patients with no appetite for tricks
    or treats, humor tasteless as chemo.
In velvet slippers, she shuffles about
    the tiny, stifling room, her tail poking folks
afraid of needles and that other place.
    Have they arrived? If not painted,
her face would still be red. Her eyes pool

the monotonous terror of Sisyphus at work,
    so Dwight, a softy, there to be unplugged,
grabs a brownie from the black cat platter
    and stashes it, when she turns her satin back,
in the fake philodendron among butts
    of cigarettes long since snuffed out.
The room inhales her absence. No one talks—
    what to say to the mirror? No one thumbs
the mound of catalogs—why buy what you've

no time for? No one reads the news mags'
   tragic tale of The Princess. For that,
they need only scan the room's shadows
   bewigged, hollow-cheeked, rouged,
they need only peruse the pink, fuzzy dome
   of the child counting her fingers
one two three. That I am healthy sickens me
   by the time nursey—no, Bubbles the Clown
in fool's regalia—motions us *Come on.*

I'm happy to stroll any yellow corridor,
   relieved to be the fourth Stooge
no one remembers. Our too-white
   Nikes squeak in concert frantic
as the Stooges' theme played at 78 rpm,
   "Three Blind Mice" befitting guys who jab
each other's eyes. Think of all their practice,
   the learning curve and sorry mishaps
getting their timing right: each thrust and block

and petulant grunt. Think of our laughing
   at pain because, for once, it's not real.
Think of Dwight thinking a finger to the eye
   or fist to the skull must be kinder than
a catheter to the heart, small pump infusing
   the larger with 5FU and Leucovorin,
names better suited to killing termites
   or unclogging a drain, which, in reverse,
his catheter is: gate through the body's

high walls, its streets pulsing within you.
   Oh my city, oh my beloved place—
oh, it's impossible to wax hieratic
   while Dwight laughs so hard he's in tears

(funny, the marriage of extremes)
    as Bubbles unplugs and caps the twin ports,
sets him free this week. She sports
    the requisite rainbow wig and floppy shoes.
When she walks her sock horn honks,

each step a bark and proclamation:
    life, life, life. . . . If not here,
what good is irony? His bitter made sweet,
    the brownies, the radiator's hissing heat,
a bald girl counting, some icing on her cheek,
    one gate opened and another slammed shut,
the embrace of sagging, butt-worn chairs—
    and wigs, a parade of wigs
as Mary casts out the devil.

Thinking of Genesis while Watching the Oscars

In the beginning there was The Beginning, and before that
the nothing from which everything has come to be something—
creation the original Hollywood production. Imagine how
the Creator preens in black jeans and turtleneck,
sporting one of those berets the French will naively believe
they invented eons hence. Angels at work on special effects,
flummoxed, ask, "He wants what?!" before dotting spots
on leopard hide, stitching the kangaroo's slouchy pouch,
before stringing wings on a feathered lizard the eagle was to be.
Nothing foils them. Not platypus nor porpoise
nor Winzahr the bay Arabian horse. Not gray whales,
peacock tails, a prairie's August swale. Good little angels,
they do what they're told: stretching the elephant's proboscis
and giraffe's ungainly neck past all heavenly proportion.
Likewise, the male organ of species *homo sapiens*—
thinking man—who'll use it to erect tall buildings
and market monster trucks in *anno Domini* 1998,
just two clicks before some say the whole shebang's
set to go in Fire or Ice—maybe both—though any Creator
ought to reserve one for next time He must annihilate
the producers of *Titanic* and The Wonder Bra for venturing
in realms of destruction and creation not rightly theirs.
What with Great Flood ruled out, He's wise to keep
options open. For no creature, not even the Creator,
will ever imagine more ways to kill than we can.

While I Burned the Autumn Garden

The fleck of ash that won't flick off, wounded
summer delivered into the arms of, well,
October. That's it, metaphor. A few clouds
in lank procession, fingering their white hankies,
and everywhere wind about to happen, poised
among the avuncular oaks like the friend
I'd trust to pick me up when my Ford's in shop,
friend who'd rescue me from the waiting room's
Field and Stream, Ammo News, the single, oily
kept-behind-the-counter *Penthouse* I once
witnessed a sixteen year old sneak off to the john.
Rescue, think of that: a collusion of
happy gods amidst our pitiful collisions,
as years ago I wrapped a tourniquet
around the arm of a guy high on LSD,
his dutiful heart arcing blood right through
the window he'd shattered to teach giggling
sorority girls a visceral lesson in anti-war decorum.
The marchers were stoned. I had no choice:
the squad car, Emergency where doctors stitched
his architect's arm and cops took names.
I learned all things have their price,
first when gratitude looped my neck like a noose,
a rope yanked tight by each *thanks, man,*
then in court for malicious property damage.
Now this lustral swoon and collapse,
this late century age of Augustus, Horace growing old
amidst the ceremony of ash and bitter wines.
All right, all right. I know Horace chastened Virgil,
"What we have no power to change,
we can learn to live with," an honorable man's lesson

in how to get by, get on. Try this then.
A singed pinch bug hauled another
through smoldering folds of pumpkin.
Oh fuck metaphor and its swayback horse:
While I burned the autumn garden,
Serb soldiers beat a man whose blood puddled
in Bosnian mud like blood puddling in mud.
I've no right to feel so powerless.

Our Armor

"Clothes make the man."

Where the sleeve cuts I've left to experts
in men's issues, say, how the break of cuff asserts
authority in this blue pinstriped looking-for-work.
To be a man is to labor with hard heart,
for cruelty is men's work, knowledge ancient
as declensions of the genitive plural, nuances
of subjunctive mood, that sorry scribe who scrawled
Vestis virum reddit and bade us remember
the chastened agent of virtue tested. And failed.
As when balding Miss Spalding, importuned
from retirement, so frantically thwacked
the black pointer on chalked verbs her teeth fell
from sunken lips not once but daily—pink debacle
jeered by the huddled offensive line and backfield
sketching dream play X's and O's
before half-ass practice they snoozed through.
Merciless, those starters and we who'd lie to be.

She stank of rank musk, or so we thought,
knowing squat of that region we'd wasted legions
of calories lusting after. She fumed at our ineptitude.
Spumes of foamy spit flecked desks nailed down
as nothing in our lives and all in hers. We hairy
howled at her gate, last castle in the kingdom
of union wage—fathers' Trojan horse, our birthright
the belly of a beast. So in season she was in season,
our weapons those we grew into: Gary's hand
that sloshed his cock around the lip of Miss Spalding's

coffee cup, 33rd straight she left class to slip
her teeth back in. Our hands that pinched
cheerleaders' cheeks so they gawked-blushed-giggled.
Hand behind the hand that shut my mouth as her lipstick
tattooed the cup of our belly-laugh, bitter grounds of cruelty—
word descended from Middle English, from the dainty French,
originally from Latin *crūdēlis, crūdēle,* "morally unfeeling,"

an inkling that comes to me now in the tri-view mirror,
the tailor dutifully asking "Dress left or right?"
so he'll measure the inseam without my flinching.
What makes a man? Can't such a fool thing be said?
Not the rope hung between his thighs,
not fist nor fart nor hairy arm. Not parts factory
nor burnt lubricant sweat. Not the mendicant
steward's pocketed pint of Beam.
Not a pencil-necked foreman grinning green.
Not the stench of smoker's bench.
Not overtime. Not the rusted lunch box
father hands to son. Not this cut of clothes.
Can't a fool say what makes a man? Speak up.
I wish I'd hollered before her lips met the cup.
I wish that huddle had kicked my chicken ass.

First Day, Container Corporation of America, June 1972

When the bleak break-room smokers asked,
   "What you run?" I answered "the half
and quarter mile," to which response

they burst in furious, gut-clutching
   yucks and howls. "No, boy," one said,
"what *machine* you run?" and I got it.

Both the joke I'd innocently made
   and the joke I was: high-school-Harry
among the balding, unionized sublime.

"Slitter 66," I said, and their blue
   ballooning guffaw burst in rarefied air,
everyone exhaling Lucky Strike at once.

Eighteen, big-haired and mutton-chopped,
   brand new black pocket tee taut over
my still tight gut, I thought they saw

the future in me and shuddered
   at their vision. Or was it their past,
themselves before the war to save

democracy—resplendent in white shirt
   and dungarees—now pot-bellied and shot?
The young think things like that.

How could I know the guy whose job I took
    came home boxed from Vietnam,
a war I fought in TV news clips

and the peace marches of us blessed
    with high draft numbers? I ate alone:
mother's cold meat loaf, bruised banana,

a Coke that gave me the jitters.
    When the horn burped, I lit out for work
like the apple polisher I'd planned to be,

though not before those men
    who'd seemed too gray had heaved me
in a tin bin of cardboard scrap

and slammed the lid, their fists beating
    rhythm to the heart thumping my throat.
Whatever republic we were then,

its pulse beat among us,
    though no one would say
the word. Sprawled headfirst

among mis-cuts and discards,
    the dross of a process I'd yet
to learn—man, this was a start.

Two

After Camelot

What authority decreed the price
   of what we want shall exceed what we can pay?
Or is it bear? From her, too, comes the ironic

gut sustenance of *want,* and later, as haltingly
   as Christmas molasses, comes the chance
beneficence of making do. Or not.

All this as it should be, for in the nest
   even the field sparrow envies the cardinal's
sharp top notch, the needle-beaked nuthatch

who walks backward, how the bunting flashes
   indigo in sun patch among shadow.
"Oh mother, not this mud brown rust and gray,"

sparrow's lament my sisters and I mimic
   for its sheer insistent ploy of annoyance
at the Kokomo Bargain Center, where

clothes too shoddy or misshapen for Kmart
   find hanger, rack, heaped table. And cheap.
"A short drive for tall savings," their jingle

as off-kilter as their fare—men's underwear
   with crotch stitched shut, dresses without neck slot,
pants with zipper in rear—an assemblage

of misbegottens from Malaysia to Jersey City
   proving the seamstress trade must be learned
by increments of mistake. As with everything.

"Look it over," my mother lectures my father,
    checking first the remnants of snipped out label
for a spared letter or logo to hint lineage

and thus quality—never mind one sleeve brushes
    the floor and the other hangs chicken wing short.
With needle and thread, things can be made right.

Such stolid, mid-American confidence
    won the great war. That, and the A-bomb.
It's dollars and cents my parents contemplate,

seated on the peeling, blue-gray radiator,
    their butt cheeks as flushed as their faces
totaling the day, hoping their math's wrong.

Beyond them snow slushes in salt and cinder
    on the wrong side of tracks a train bellows down
every 45 or so, asbestos sifting the warehouse

with each diesel lurch and belch, so the wall
    between in and out seems a lie of unlimited
possibility. Here, three days before Christmas 1963,

our Catholic president entombed beneath
    his sputtering flame, Camelot in shambles.
My kid sister sets up household below

a rack of London Fog reject trench coats.
    Her butterfly glasses lift from her face,
white and lilting in the half-light of dream.

She's married her suddenly articulate bear
    who promised the world and got her this
far, where it's my job to watch her now that

my teenage sister has slouched to the Chevy
    in fear she'd be seen. By whom, an hour from home?
And here, wouldn't they bear equal shame?

Here, among the making do, blithely
    untinged by rage, not a soul extolling
"those who have naught, have much that can't be bought"—

some chime to make you feel better, as, in fact,
    money does: the biblical clink of pocketed shekels
straightening the crooked back, slicking the hair,

springing the step of those who hum its tune.
    Feel better. As in, money makes you
feel better than those without any,

though to say so is as un-American
    as believing Santa will bring your stuff wrapped
in last year's paper, spritzed here and there

with tape tears and the white snag of tag
    beneath tag, a name crossed out. You'll learn
who's on top matters, the necessary lie we live by.

Poem Buried within a Time Capsule to Be Unearthed Spring 2097

Citizens, what did you find
   when awakened this morning?

Your sky as blue as ours,
   a few sparrows rustling
among lime-green leaves
   of April maples?
All people fed
   and housed and free?

This would be the great blessing—
   though a still greater surprise.

Home Economics

If not the Betty Crocker commercial,
    then the smell of vanilla extract,
an oven timer slicing kitchen quiet:

    something to trapdoor a winter afternoon
beneath memory's ornate noose
    which is, alas, a noose nonetheless.

To put my neck in is to feel the clock's tick tock,
    the porch knocker clacking,
to be the boy jerking open the oak door

    for impeccable Mr. Burke,
tanned above polished loafers topped off with dimes.
    He's come for this week's cake,

devil's food with chocolate icing
    spritzed to resemble the sailboat
he floats the murky lake in—Lady Luck,

    all teak and brilliant brass.

Mother tents an Eisenhower hair net
    over her bouffant—
cleanliness as style and substance.

    She bakes other folks' cakes, pies, cookies.
No one says *women's work.*
    No one has to.

This morning, her son poured a proud cloud of flour,
    broke the yolk blood streaked through.
He stirred and fidgeted, prayed bleak rain

    would crack to sun and endless ball games.
You, oh son oblivious to this necessarily secondary drama
    of your youth,

I'd like a word with you.

Boy, what are you thinking
    when you tote the tin cake pan
to the car for a lousy nickel's tip,

    your peach-fuzz cheek pinched pink?
What don't you see when the crisp five passes
    his hand to hers?

She cracks her Ball jar hoard
    not for mink or pearls
but day-old bread and Mrs. Paul's Fish Sticks—

    the dreck poor Catholics choke down.

Boy with ants in his pants, look me in the eye.
    Ask what she thinks
of home economics—her eyes rocking

    from sink to cheap clock
chiming your father home from work?
    How graceful she makes this waltz

with ball and chain, with love.
    Boy, sleepily square,
oh son oblivious: Wake up, wake up.

Politics of Mop and Sponge

Because it sickens her, she scrubs
    the toilet last—necessity's habit
        as apt as those uniform hose
            she buys in Phar-Mor dozens,

parking lot crammed with more Chevies
    than cars in all of Sarajevo,
        where her husband and father *poof*
            disappeared, sniper's black magic havoc

among pocked walls grinning
    gap-toothed like the devil who took
        them from her. That she died too,
            waters crossed only to find Peoria,

belies the afterlife: cleaning the Sleep King
    and its pink honeymoon rooms,
        velour haunt of Hunt truckers
            and the twins from Big Al's strip joint

who favor the pun Suite 69.
    There, each noon the manager kindly
        inquired how she liked her job
            and just what could she do

about his tented crotch—
    implying hard connections—
        so she agreed to a hand-job, though
            wouldn't remove the yellow rubber glove

she'd cleaned the grubby tub with
   and Tilex raised blisters his wife wanted
      answers for, which was the weeping end
         of that. She's Black Madonna

of Spic and Span, around whom bloom
   ashtray votives, pink lipstick hickeys,
      green hockers wreathed about the trash
         no one can hit amidst the unearthly

din of the wake-up call, amidst
   the rose a lover opens to say
      yes, yes upon the bedspread she'll
         later unrumple to discover

a sodden surprise. Last New Year's
   she'd found black bra and garters,
      three liters of Cold Duck still chilled
         in sink, razor blade and coke mirror

bitter with white powder. It's
   a wash this Valentine's Day, lone
      plastic crocus and basketball
         on color TV she swivels to watch

while mopping the bath, where last
   she bends to scrub the toilet, where
      last her husband's face stares back
         among the E. coli and the crap

she flushes down, where last she gently
   loops a slip around the seat,
      to signal it's safe—the Lysolled throne
         now *Sanitized for Your Protection.*

To the Bookstore Manager Who Stuffs
Each Purchase with a *How to Get a Refund* Bookmark

We wonder if this sends the right message,
if the book might yet be loved despite its flaws,

as we love the one we marry and the family
married into—how she hums Brahms

over breakfast, for instance, or the way
he runs the faucet while brushing his teeth—

not to mention Uncle Lowell's gratuitous
flatulence, Auntie Em's concrete fruitcake.

Might not these gifts (who says flaws?) teach us
love greater than the ease of giving

back what first does not please? Our petty
presumptions grow haughty when bereft

of responsibility—Oh, that Jew whose beard
we'd trim, a black woman ripe of cheap sachet,

the blotchy white kid nearly as nervous
as his zits—can't we take them back, exchange

this world we can't fathom for another?
Trying is so trying, isn't it?

Take heart. We have one.
We don't tattoo return instructions

on each plump newborn's plump wrist. Not yet.
This life gurgles in a tongue we've forgotten.

This voice in our night begs us, *Listen.*

Because You're American

You love the hum of a well-oiled engine about to turn 200,000,
    camera on bucket seat
to shoot the ticker at 199,999.9, AM news announcing
    the Philippines has named
a golf course in honor of John Paul II, not because the pope plays
    but because his helicopter
landed there and thus consecrated eighteenth green and clubhouse bar
    you're half a globe away from,
wheeling through big bluestem, oak, and black locust to (no kidding)
    grandma's house
beside the bridge where now an exultation of white pelicans drifts
    the Des Moines River,
central Iowa sudden late March exotic and you in wonder of America,
    what with pelicans in Iowa
and bolus doses of vitamin C said to restore smokers' tarry lungs,
    though more research is needed
to explain why white pelicans fish cooperatively like good little Marxists,
    line up to beat their wings
upon the water and drive fish to shallows for easy dining, a process
    which to your amazement
they've begun while the car clicks 200,000.2, the camera in hand
    to snap the pelicans
in full collective display as the moment fritters away to Stephen Stills
    singing "Deja Vu"
so why not pull off to catch the pelicans sparkling like crystal shards
    in a punch bowl,
though a guy with arm crutch clutters the foreground and it's best to wait
    until he clears the shot
but he won't any time soon, left crutch plodding, right arm reaching back
    to yank right leg,

shoulders and hips lurching to swivel and shudder his body ahead.
  Because this is America,
the engine strums its oiled strings at a buck twenty-five a gallon,
  Barry Manilow oozes
from the single muffled speaker, and the guy with crutch has earned a yard,
  maybe two,
his face a proud saucer of water. There's "Chilly Billy" broadcasting
  from I-80's new HoJo,
free mugs and tee shirts, free rooms for seniors who've lost a spouse.
  Because this is America,
there's stale Doublemint in the glove box, a black man in a Jeep stopping
  by the guy with crutch,
who shakes his head, flaps his arm, then waves "Go on, go on" till the Jeep
  launches gravel
like the missiles that protect us. There's grandma waiting, teens squealing
  tickets to "Independence Day,"
DJ swearing he owns photos that prove we're not alone. There's "Deja Vu"
  all over again
on Double Play Tuesday, joke as obscene as Stills' singing at Woodstock II.
  Because this is America,
and you're American, you love the guy who reaches back to yank his leg,
  oh blessings, white pelicans in Iowa.

Juliet Prowse and the Cast of *Can-Can* Dance for Nikita Khrushchev, Hollywood, 1959

Descending through thunderheads, he'd ordered
    his pilot twice to circle the block letters,
heal-all white on a dry hillside—*puny,*

he'd thought, the whole sad charade nowhere
    bigger than life. While his motorcade stalls
and traffic gawks, she ponders her part

in cold war drama. Sinatra, her co-star, suggests,
    "Think of him buck naked. It'll still
your jitters." She pukes in her pink trash can.

Then sirens and Secret Service, Mr. and Mrs. K
    parade to chairs their names are stenciled on.
The Mrs., stout potato, nearly topples

the liquored-up chivalric director
    who offers his hand. Some garbled Russian,
an automatic bow, Khrushchev appraising

the best pair of legs since Grable's as mere
    bomber art. Halfway through, she floats home,
adolescent ballerina dancing

Swan Lake her first time, only to return
    to Khrushchev, spectacles on, ogling her
panties' ruffled crotch flash up, down, up.

Applause, his cheeks flushed above burnished teeth,
    and the Mrs., now silent potato,
beads sweat along a not-so-faint mustache.

So much pleads future tense: Khrushchev's rant
    against such evident Western decadence
splashing newspapers the lurid world over,

a photo of their handshake so ubiquitous
    even Elvis, who never reads, decides
at a glance she'll play his love in *G.I. Blues.*

Nyet. No, not yet. Push rewind. Not the late
    jumpsuited and bulbous Elvis stoned on stage
in Vegas. Rewind. Not Oswald dropping

on knee to squeeze the trigger on Camelot.
    Not even Kennedy and the missiles
of October. There, oh sun-drenched

Eisenhower afternoon, sea breeze sweetly
    buffeting white taffeta. Sinatra
mixes double martinis—one for him,

one for her taut legs knotted as the curtain
    she changes behind—Frankie confiding,
"Baby, I think the guy really dug it."

That Other Four Letter F-Word the Gods So Love

Sure fame enthralls us. That's easy.
    What of those who finger the beaded glass
but never get to drain it, say, Pete Meyers,
    Michael Jordan's cobwebbed backup,
or Yankee Wally Pipp, who rested one
    and sat thereafter as the Iron Horse rode
2,130 straight? What busted justice recasts
    your name as verb: to be "Wally Pipped"
a fate that befalls the displaced lazy.
    What to make of offbeat Pete Best,
the Beatles' drummer drummed out
    before the yeah yeah yeahs, the mop hair
and weak-kneed teens, who thus gave us Ringo,
    Sgt. Pepper, everything up to and including
the shrunken conductor of "Shining Time Station"
    my four year old thinks sweet but a fool,
proving again all Ringo has to do is
    "Act Naturally." What of those lucky
just to wait fame's table for lousy tips
    or clean the foul Gehenna john?
What did Warhol know of their fifteen minutes?

I like to think of the unsuspecting
    in Roethke's University of Washington
poetry workshop about the time
    Elvis rocked Sun in Memphis.
Imagine the innocents fond of "poesy."
    Imagine them sweetly leafing the week's
dazzler by Carolyn Kizer or Dick Hugo.

Imagine them scanning James Wright's
sonnets of scorned murderer and hapless drunk.
    How library school must've reclaimed its luster!
What became of those—the serious
    and the dilettantes? Were they jealous,
as all poets not so secretly are,
    or blessedly bemused, assured the world's
most cynical oxymoron is "Famous Poet"?
    What if I—not famous for magnanimity—
braced the fabled Seattle table
    Wright crooned Goethe's lyrics upon?
What tepid brew would I have sipped,
    seated eye level at the proverbial feet?

On my desk, I've a snapshot of Wright,
    John Knoepfle, John Logan, and Robert Bly
gathered, circa 1960, at Bly's Minnesota farm.
    By then ELVIS had made all caps.
This photo's the poetry Rorschach,
    a test of literary ambition.
Pondering it, poets score the four
    like Bandstand's Rate-a-Record: who's hot,
who's not, who's hit the Norton's Top 40,
    who's faintly quaint as Paul Anka
or this scallop-edged black and white.
    In the photo, they mill around
a back porch door, sunny afternoon,
    unruly bushes spilling over a knee-high
picket fence. They've big tumblers in hand,
    Bly a leaf? a poem? in one of his.
Wearing their faces young, three
    look over their drinks as if to ask,
"What is this bitter, this sweet?"
    His glass already downed, Wright stands
at rear, one step off the steps he'd soon ascend,
    and looks out over others' shirted shoulders

toward something he squints at, something
   incandescent his last gulp delivered
a vision of, as well as the first slim crease
   of smile or grimace on his still smooth face
whose lines he's about to earn one by one.

Sales

Okay it was need lifted his feet into the van,
    post summer-of-love summer 1970,
not the thought of his service to humanity
    introducing cable television to Hoosiers
in the land before CNN or Nicklelodeon,

in ancient days before 24-hour classic reruns
    were either. It was five bucks per sign up,
all cash and no taxes. It was underage beer
    and cheap hotels, headboard banging
as the bosses celebrated each day's take

with capitalist *Kama Sutra.* It was peanut butter
    and jelly his mother packed, pocketfuls
of Wheaties and hotel mints, any way to save
    for Soc 101, Lit & Comp, reading Nietzsche
on maple-shaded lawn tennis afternoons.

It was Lawrenceville's river distillery,
    Seagrams corn squeezings blending air
that burnt his nose and stuffed townfolks' billfolds
    with paychecks he'd hook with the lure
of La-Z-Boy decadence the Joneses couldn't resist.

Oh my, it was miles of roof antennae—tilting,
    shingle-leaking—an above-ground, wind-riven
gold mine, his own three channel vein
    of ghost reception waiting to be worked clean.
It was a hundred bucks a day, easy.

Then too there were stories his buddies told.
   The divorcee dusting lonely in lace teddy,
bending over way too often, reaching up up up,
   how she fingered the Hoover's pale handle
and flipped its switch with electric pout.

Or the skinny-dipping twins with mom gone
   shopping two towns over, the temp near 90
and what to do but join their Coppertone rubs,
· their Bacchic grapes and poolside Polaroids
lost in the sadly clichéd back gate escape.

All he got were grannies with walkers, bald guys
   in torn boxers snoozing through games. Once
he turned tables on Jehovah's Witnesses, giving
   his spiel with foot in *their* door. Even then he paid:
an hour fretting *The Watchtower* before they'd sign.

It was money, all money—until the round face
   at the split level kindly asked him in
the velvet living room and brought a Coke with lime
   to mask its bitter pill. The man with Dutch-boy
Sonny Bono hair talked and hunted his wallet,

talked and fumbled for a fountain pen, talked
   as he left the room only to return
with checkbook tented over his red brick
   erection. "Take it," he said—or was it, asked?—
his face a smorgasbord of greasy need.

He wondered what it would be to take
   or be taken like that, a shudder of wonder
with seismic aftermath, though strangely
   it's not that he most recalls but the poodle
yapping at the patio door, yap yap yapping,

and the echo, like a poodle dropped down
    some far canyon begging to come home,
and his own volcanic laugh at the thought—
    a French poodle down the Grand Canyon!—
belly laughing, arms flailing so wildly

a brass lamp crashed and popped its bulb.
    When he tossed his Coke bottle football
to black velvet Elvis open and calling for it,
    the man ran to let the dog in and push
the boy out, handing him a wad of money—

not for sex, which didn't happen—
    but for cable. Sixteen channels, no snow.
Yeah, maybe to buy his silence, even though
    the Dutch-boy man had little to fear:
What guy would share this story with his pals?

What a fool he'd been. What he let himself,
    for an instant, imagine. No, he stumbled
to a park with swings and merry-go-round,
    humid air Seagrams bittersweet—
the perfect convergence to match his age—

and found a shaded picnic table
    to sleep away an American afternoon
beneath hardwood maple and hickory,
    flea bane and tickweed winking at his feet.
Good night, sweet prince. Good night.

When they roused him to board the VW van,
    a pink sunset slunk about his ankles,
his disheveled, Coke-spotted bell bottoms.
    When they passed the squat, burnt-rope joint,
he refused, befitting the letterman he was

and would remain, a couple years anyway.
    When finally they tallied the day's sales—
he, an industry pioneer—had only the one
    and a yapping headache, though he promised
tomorrow he'd do better, and did.

Full Moon at Tree Line, San Juan Range, Colorado

That battered flashlight strung inside
the tent, small sun on a rope, lurches over
wife and daughter and son, then back again,
tracing a shrinking arc across their placid faces.
In the dark, I wonder what life awaits them,
what death? Surely the hour and the altitude
make me as ponderous as the émigré poet
whose village burned beneath Nazi parachutes.
The hour and the altitude, or some perversion
of the saying my father's father spoke
at every funeral but his own,
"I'll confess to guilt for my good fortune,
if you'll admit to hating me for both,"
spreading guilt like jam over peanut butter.
Among stunted pines, a coyote asks, "Who, who?"
and others answer, accusingly, "You, you,"
though death imagined as peanut butter
on white is not the metaphor of an émigré poet,
only lunch at tree line above boulder fields
sprinkled with mine tailings, sulfurous tongues
spilling down ridge where Alfred Packer,
ignoring Chief Ouray's advice, led his party
into the one-way mountains of October.
Snowbound, they died and Alfred ate them,
walked out next June with a sickly grin.
"It's sweet," he said, "like young chicken."
Now restaurants feature *The Packer:*
chicken breast with pickles fingered
around the bun. This, we call marketing.
This explains why I want something to die for.
A revolution. Something larger than the pitiful

cloud my breath makes. I want North Korea
to ban the bomb, Iraq to embrace its Kurds,
Jesse Helms to dance with Carol Moseley-Braun.
Really I want to sleep, but the flashlight
pours its small cascade while a spider drops
her skein as if riding the beam's particle and wave,
the sloshing of body against body that accounts
for these sleeping children I want to protect
from the hour and the altitude and spider bite.
Yet *want* is surely the problem, our appetite
as keen as the spider's, all of us
spinning beneath light hung on a rope,
under the dome that thrums with every breath
each of us takes and takes and takes.

Logos

"Hi, I'm Bob," each elevator name tag bragged—
    not Robert or Rob or Bobby,
  but Bob as in Newhart, as in aged Coach Knight,

as in Packwood, our groper senator. Befuddled,
    we beheld the convention we'd hitched-on,
  this bevy of Bobs celebrating Bob-ness in Peoria.

Amid back-slapping and plaid pants, blue blazers,
    loafers and a sea of comb-overs, the Ballroom,
  you might say, bobbed in polyester waves.

Deb, pregnant with son, bore their solicitous
    furies: "Name him Bob, and he'll make our
  newsletter cover," its headline puffery:

Elevator Membership Drive Rides Success.
    O how the propped open doors beckoned
  us to be Bob and wife-of-Bob, delirious

with friends, as was the high school me
    with fake ID before cops spied my haul
  of toilet paper, the can of beets, a warm case

of sale-priced Stroh's. Before the dowdy clerk
    shook her crooked finger, clucking,
  "The beets were a dead giveaway, boy!"

The fake ID was Joe Slotsky's, smash mouth
    fullback whose daddy called him "Sue"
  after that Johnny Cash tune. We teased "Sexy Suzy"

in our goal-line huddle, and he smacked opponents
    in lieu of daddy. Weekends
  I became Joe, my middle name—my grandfather's,

my father's, my young son's first.
    I sported platform shoes and three-day stubble.
  I grunted a lot. I chewed toothpicks.

On weekends hip brickhouse girls phoned me up
    when parents skipped town
  so they might carpet white rooms with booze.

They named me Cool Daddy and The Breeze,
    and I became the things they made of me.
  Why not Bob? Those doors gaped like gates

to Paradise—as if Eden's first couple
    named every earthly thing Bob: *See the Bob*
  with regal mane, See the beautiful Bobs gallop,

See that humming-Bob flit amidst flowering Bob.
    How sweet to think the all and every
  bound by some cosmic order, as if Logos

had only good intentions and we did too,
    brother and sister. Oh no, we make meaning
  and thus name what we can't fathom.

Go tell nigger, tell spic, tell any honky.
    In naming resides power no Greek reason
  elides. Tell fag and dyke. To name a thing

says less of what it is than what it isn't.
      Tell fatso, tell shorty, go tell the whore.
    Tell the four-eyed fool poet who thinks

he thinks this first. Blessed or cursed,
      naming names the namer. Tell Marley,
    yes, Bob, who thought the worst of us gods.

Three

Fishing Naked

Bent knee within the cathedral
   of Indian summer, I canoed Crooked Creek's
     great nave adorned with Paduan gold

rich as Giotto's *Lamentation,* where
   Christ-become-man becomes spirit again,
     one body broken among angels' keening.

Alone, I was bamboozled by the sheer
   luxuriance of decay, opulence of loss
     as robed as Catholic pageantry

I'd skipped out of, having swallowed
   Emerson from ullage to last dregs
     of final exam. I was adrift,

lost amidst Emerson's theorizing
   all language is fossilized metaphor,
     pondering the sere bone source

of a word upon my tongue—"paddle"—
   which, in the world of the real,
     simply blistered my hands

as I slogged from here to there,
   where the old couple was fishing,
     their bodies as naked and drooping

as the bent catalpa they lay beneath,
   its brown pods dangling limp dicks.
     I cleaved to the bank. Sure, to look:

I didn't know the crotch grayed,
   breasts withered and hung,
      his sex dark as old hemp rope.

I didn't know much.
   How to get by them, for instance,
      fishing naked in sluiced light,

without plundering their pleasure,
   or hooking the eye of my enlightenment:
      backwater-transparent-eyeball-Peeping-Tom.

◇ ◇ ◇

What is there about pleasure and its
   perpetual imperilment, the clock
      tick ticking, the hand about to knock,

a galaxy of telephones and yours
   bound to ring as soon as you slip
      in bed, in bath, in the folds of some

all-afternoon casserole whose cheeses
   grow bitter when cold? What is there
      about pleasure brevity makes sweeter,

the way Saturday's blushed pears
   become Sunday's dozen gone to mush?
      Why is the water slide's wait

decades longer than its ride,
   time enough to dot-to-dot
      every freckled shoulder?

What is there about pleasure
   best-sellers must counsel us
      slow down, take it easy—

the dance with silken hand,
  good wine beside tall candles,
    your lover unzipped by pursed lips?

◇ ◇ ◇

Pleasure, like speech, makes us human.
  Or so we like to think,
    forgetting we choose pleasure

less often than it chooses us.
  To choose or be chosen:
    either way's delicious,

though guilt's greedy fingers
  clutch the scant throat
    all pleasure sallies in and out of.

We call cats' purring mere reflex,
  dogs' humping simply Darwinian!—
    because we do the deed when not in heat,

thus confusing pleasure with the story
  of who couldn't refuse the proffered apple.
    Neither one, lest you forget,

as did a friend who phoned us over
  to witness paired primordial bugs
    mating behind her stove clock's glass,

oblivious in their Bermuda
  of honeymoon dreams
    made tropical by hot pot roast.

Blissful, if bliss is something
  bugs can feel, they went at it,
    secure beyond the timer's needle arm

until the lady of the house ballpeened
    her stove clock—glass shards,
        severed legs, two red armored heads

spicing the uncovered pan
    of corn she tossed out back
        for the dog to cut his tongue on.

                    ◇ ◇ ◇

Who says the real fount
    of pleasure resides below the waist
        or among the mind's crinkles, and not

on the tongue—who gets the best
    of both—lord of his temple,
        honored guest in others'?

Think of sodden places the tongue goes,
    brave emissary of our heart,
        sampling others' breath and spunk

to bring back unspeakable riches.
    Think of all who visit bearing wine
        and ale, flesh of pear or apple,

assembled culinary delights
    whose sight and scent promise nothing
        without the blessing of taste.

This, our simple ceremony
    of the ravished and thus exalted.
        This, the communion of tongue

and other by which a world
    enters us. O, isn't this the spot
        we enter the world—

not in body but in thought
   given body? Speak a word
      (simple chemical, firing neurons)

and idea bodies forth beyond our lips.
   If not in language, where else
      the juncture of mind and flesh?

That's why, cloistered in a doctor's
   stifling office, I admit to heady pleasure
      just looking at jarred tongue depressors.

Once oaken trunk, supple maple,
   stolid ash branch—now autoclaved
      for safety—they yearn for the sordid,

fecund life of my tongue or yours:
   one quick touch, a throaty *ahhhhhh,*
      that unceremonious toss to trash.

          ◇ ◇ ◇

Degas at midlife, roughly where I am,
   tossed Impressionism in the can.
      He loathed his worldly reputation

as "Degas, the painter of perfect dancers,"
   and so undid himself. He drew nudes
      gravity had had its sweet way with,

plump and rounded, lumpy-thighed:
   years of pan drippings,
      goat butter, cheeses as pungent

and unforgiving as any rival's eye.
   Now, now, his pencil consoled,
      sketching models at bath with sponge,

hair spooled in curtains of velveteen
    curls—women rapt by the toilette's
        casual ritual of appraisal and repair.

Such was Degas' pleasure, sketching
    from the rear so every rump bloomed
        without the furious complications

a face unfurls. In "After the Bath,"
    a charcoal figure (I'll say, Degas)
        flips a towel's oceanic waves toward

a bather, her body's flushed vessel at rest
    on the tub's cool lip. Both his hands,
        nearly erased, and hers, blurred

with motion, plead *This isn't me*—
    amid crosshatch ticking toward night,
        the liquid dark all things drain to.

                    ◇   ◇   ◇

"All is water," Thales pronounced,
    the first recorded philosophical
        utterance. Who will disagree,

cast amidst October's waves,
    leaves swelling from elm and locust,
        a priestly ash, one squat burr oak

the kids' swing sails upon?
    Listen, the principal foundation
        of Western thought is itself fluid,

wanting nothing more than to change
    its state—vapor, cloud, rain,
        then river and ocean again, again.

Wanting nothing more than to get
   from one place to another
      as wildly as we run to catch

a leaf before it touches down,
   grounded and thus claimed
      as we must be, will be, are.

Wanting nothing more than to be
   the fallen who does not fall,
      one carried with fanfare

to the great table—itself, in former life,
   oak-with-leaves. Wanting to be
      propped among frost-stung mums

beside paired candles, the one
   anointed by beeswax and the sour
      hurried breath of dinner prayer.

Wanting nothing more than to be
   the one saved who sprawls
      to dust in our own good time.

◇ ◇ ◇

From dust you came, the story goes,
   though I think it's more likely water,
      this pivotal confusion wrought by a single

sadly flawed translation. Or maybe it's
   all ornamental, the source and end of us
      less in the thing than in the changing of one

to another, pleasure as blessed
   as any stranger become lover become
      wife become poem about same.

"Blindfold a metaphysician, and he'll
    lead you to water," brooded Melville,
        who nonetheless hated Emerson's

insufficient appreciation of evil.
    That was before Emerson's mind went,
        and solids like *table, cup, chair* became

Platonic things he had no words for,
    no tongue to speak them. It was Plato,
        after all, who thought male and female

once joined, now severed, thus sex our quest
    to reunite. Lead a metaphysician
        to water, blindfold him, and he'll drown

in pleasure of a thing neither solid nor gas
    though partly both. This is pleasure
        we have no language for, only articulate bodies

yearning for change, vertiginous
    along the shifting line water and shore unmake,
        all of us fishing that pleasurable edge.

Four

In Thanks of Visitations

To imagine is to fathom the lie as truth, a notion half-drunk
    and veering home
with headlights off, the blearily righteous eye Degas made peace with:
    "We see what
we want to see, and in this falsification comes art." Edgar isn't here
    to explain how
black-capped chickadees, lacquered in Monday sunlight, can dot an oak
    we chainsawed down
when we built-on for the surprise son who contrived to arrive with
    his mother's cancer—
no time to be unexpected, she expecting the worst amidst nurses'
    crisp whites,
a surfeit of beeps and bongs, limp petals of Muzak, this din crescendoing
    like a Wal-Mart stereo
unhinging its cringing speakers as well as the dry-rotted sash and window lintel.
    Ah, shut it off.
"Lacquered in Monday sunlight" we know to mean bright, highlighted
    as in a painting
we think most real because it's not—only a painted bird on painted branch
    in painted sunlight,
all of us gushing *She looks so alive,* as we say of the casketed dead
    whom we aspire
to make lifelike, though no one who's kissed their chill lips is ever again
    so fooled,
as no one hospitalized is hoodwinked by marketing the place as "home-
    away-from-home."
That's the way of it, stranger in foreign land, clutching an insurance passport,
    a duffel of clothes,
phrases parroted to close with *thank you, doctor* inflected as if posing
    a question
no one will answer in English. That's the way of it, to be the Other

beneath a single shock

of oak snapped off so we napped under the home tree, only to awaken
   fitful and pilfering,

ten minutes sleep courtesy of an *Alien Update* left behind by one
   practiced in the need

to believe, say, "The Pope's Clandestine Encyclical on Alien Life":
   Papal plea

to treat all aliens with respect we reserve for our earthly fellows
   and his pledge

to save the little green souls of those little green beings God made
   in His image

as He's made us, an otherworldly propagation of faith promising a true
   Universal religion.

Oh faith: to believe these things come to us, that they visit
   in cool of night

or broad daylight of our windswept lives, waving small hands,
   faces beaming

as if they'd feasted on light—as I awakened to the hospital nun
   dousing wife and son

with holy water blessed by a bishop whose oddly mitered cap looms,
   in retrospect,

vaguely alien. She touched a finger to their brows wet with night sweat,
   then lifted it

to her pursed lips. Tasting what? Maybe salt or telltale sickness,
   the tepid confection

she'd splashed them with, surely something as unexpected as this boy,
   lacquered in Monday sunlight,

branches tucked in each sleeve and arced from his coat's throat—
   an image we know

to mean boy-as-tree beneath the metaphor-as-tree that, I'll admit,
   we didn't cut down.

There I lied, as Degas implies in service of truth all art lies, which itself is true,
   as is the part

about mother and son, her cancer, their recovery figured in these chickadees,
   black-habited nuns

who've come to bless the feeder strung across my son's breath-held chest,
   all true.

70

March, Where the Kickapoo Bends

"I hope I die before I get old."
—The Who

Three of us walked, though that
   was hardly all, down white-

tail path through bracken wood,
   oak and hickory, track

of elms disease had wracked
   and left to stand, bark peeling

from wood the color of bone,
   all home for woodpecker

and later sweet fodder
   for morel. Three of us

walked, though that was hardly
   all, down past a rusting

woodstove, bright heaps of glass
   and stone, the lone jack-in-

the-pulpit rising like sex
   after sixty. Three of us walked—

one who'd patched his marriage,
   one who'd found a job, one

whose wife and son had slipped
cancer's grip—down through damp

folds of Solomon's seal,
both false and real, through May

Apple's raised umbrellas
and multiflora rose

someone's good intentions
had made tangled pest, down

to the Kickapoo bend,
a bluff of osage-orange,

down where bluebells bloomed
ground to sky and our steps

flushed a chorus of doves
whose wings burst feathered

laughter. Down where bells
rang our silent thanks—

warm beer as explosive
as middle-age we once

blithely swore we'd refuse.

Little Puddles, Spring Buckets, the Earth Awash

with bees, green tea leaves and sassafras,
   garden mint so pungent the shut window
      can't shut it out—we lie there,

bathed in sweet wet breath of angels
   who envy our lips' blessed rush of flesh
      on flesh they must turn their eyes from

in pain of their own want of a body
   we step out of when making love,
      vessel we hover above in spent moments,

so sweetly deep we've thrashed to come
   out this other side, flushed and astonished
      to have plucked ourselves free of want:

pink, hardy weed whose roots sprout
   among puddles on breast and belly
      and thigh—tomorrow's lubricious blossom.

On Landscapes, or Cutting My Son's Hair at the Kitchen Sink

The first snip—like his first word—
    so muddled and misshapen
  what follows tries to be corrective
in the quick way hands have with language,

mute dialect of head and heart. Think of all
    he'll say with *his* hands: knuckled fist
  or postgame shake, the first caressed breast.
Think of all the coming and going, his waves

to beckon or relinquish, all the fingers
    pointed in anger or joy, as now, he gestures
  toward the owl's feather nested in burr oak leaf,
prize he hat-hid from woods to house

past unsuspecting parents. "Feather," he says.
    No, a word slurred with "f" and "r,"
  a jumble of phonemes that might be anything—
even "father"—if I hadn't seen him point.

After all, one hears what one wants to hear,
    which explains why I always look up
  "pulchritude," unconvinced anything so ugly
can mean *beautiful,* let alone *comely.*

Oh feather and leaf my son sneaked in,
    pummeled by Nerf ball, chewed on by cats,
  sudden boat in dishwater sea,
the landscape we move through moves also

through us, inner and outer weather
    tongue and hand speak to, silent or not.
    Suppose one sees what one wants to see.
Despite that lovely lie, the tree's still there

to smack your head upon. Say there's
    comeliness of the physical being
    and of that other one, owls amidst dark
we see but don't see. Be glad of that.

And this: brushing a boy's blond hair,
    feathering a cowlick that won't lie down,
    charged as if by some keener need.
There's a world my hands will never touch.

What I Hate about Postmodernism

As sunrise percolated through spires
of black oak, my son has flung banana slices
on the window, so from his angle
the sun's gold face has eyes as off kilter
as Klee's "Head of a Man"—a model perhaps
for Klee's befuddled father at 6:02 A.M.,
or Klee thinking of being a father,
one eye focused on joy at hand, the other
on some distant vision of white shoes,
white belt and hat. The End.
Because it's morning the radio's mostly talk,
though the local radio personality slathers
something vaguely obscene over my cold toast.
Six foot six and a mere 142 pounds, he's "Fatman"—
and thus Postmodern. His name, he says, bespeaks
the "irrevocable breach between sign and signified."
He's a gas, as is the fiery thing we signify
by "sun," shedding its first rays on the painting
bought after my glasses snapped and skittered
across polished hardwood: bare bulbs
sudden opulent moons, night a thick smudge
spackled with crinolines. I held a lens to one eye,
then the next, like my diabolical Other's monocle,
shifting feet before a three-piece composition
whose every edge aligns so there's no right
way to hang it. No wrong way either,
as my friend explained, in the loft he shares
with a stunning fiction writer. She,
though not his lover, writes each morning
in the nude so he might sketch her breasts
at rest on the formica tabletop's lip.

Over coffee and onion bagels, at first
they looked a couple, but he was too solicitous
with cream and she with lumps of sugar,
and the newspaper was there only to line
the kitty-litter box, Sunday bra and panty ads
to sketch thin necks, arched thighs.
You think I've gone on, that my lingering over
their marijuana plants propped in wall-high windows
hints of envy—though it's not the fact
but the *idea* of growing pot in windows
which seduces me, that recklessness.
What is envy anyway but the admission
of something absent in your life
you hope to find in the anything of another's,
simple longing devolved into the primary colors
of want blotched across this painting:
the red splotch a cardinal feeding two monstrous
cowbird chicks, their necks raised high
above the bird's scrawny and doomed brood,
his good intentions nothing more than reason
subjugated by pride. And what is pride
but the first sin: an apple of ineffable
loveliness hollowed by bees, and this
a fool's vision. The Beginning.
Be honest: You thought the snapped glasses
were a metaphor. They were just cheap,
a bargaining with gods as redemptive as sun
parting sky to reveal what's already there
though I could not see it—the world's gift,
supple and forgiving at any father's hour.

Late Valentine, with Daisies

How not to think of love, entering
   Blackbeard's Floral Ship Shoppe
to "Louie, Louie" playing on WMXP

93.3 FM, "All Louie, All the Time,"
   where only a DJ's poorly recorded
sophomorics spell our need for order.

Surely the owners must be out to lunch,
   abandoning their floral ship to a crew
of Gen-Xers in baggy jeans and cropped tops

cranking the ultimate garage band song
   so seductively even the door buzzer
can't be heard above the din, and who

at such moment dances with eyes open?
   The sign says *Ring Bell for Service*
though I won't, having two minutes

to indulge an anthem to pleasures
   only hormone-engorged teenagers
make out amidst the mythic muddle

shouted into the lone mic strung
   twelve feet above the drunken Kingsmen:
state of the art recording, circa 1963.

Ah history's got a good beat and you
   can dance to it, even if you don't know
Richard Berry sold "Louie, Louie" for a mere

$500 bucks to flip side "You Are My Sunshine,"
   how the tune languished in a Tacoma 10-cent
record bin till Rockin' Robin Roberts reworked

a version the Kingsmen later covered,
   whose out-of-focus vocals convinced us
the lyrics were obscene; how that rumor shot

the song to *Billboard*'s #2 and led the feds
   to a padded room to spin the platter
first fast then s-l-o-w enough to conclude

the lyrics were "unintelligible at any speed"—
   confirming no one over thirty gets it.
An *it* we two swaddled in the thrice-a-week

sheets of our college bed, beside
   the burnished urn, the cinnamon candles,
incense wreathed above a turntable's

vaulted altar. There we'd bear youth's Grail
   and Bowl, we'd wear the fated talisman.
We'd swear our sweaty vows beneath its

cryptic lyrics, reedy three-cord organ
   so hypnotic even now Blackbeard's
back room letter-stuffers sway like weeds

in the fluorescent wash of its tidal pull.
   Framed by the door's lit portal,
two of them wail "Lou—ee, Lou—I,"

their lips parting sea. They smile, they dance.
   They lick envelopes with rhythmic grace
though the song halts and starts over

for the twentieth time this hour, the plodding
    postmodern irony of *classic rock* lost
among lyrics so malleable you make them

anything you want. As once, my love,
    you named yourself a garden, braided daisies
in your hair, then sweetly let me in.

Yesterday

Never mind that. Tax forms and fudged receipts.
Numbers' work is despair, as when a lover begins,
"Let me count the ways," the sum sets no fruit,
her roots in clay. This time I'll dawdle in lawn chair
amidst the plum's yawn of bloom and wonder
which is more to bear: blossom or kept promise,
the keeping or the dropping away? When we met,
I played Mercutio and you the beguiling Juliette
romanced by some twit with ladder and tights.
Swordplay in verse. Jealousy. Sot of borrowed wit,
I died, spilling "But 'tis enough, 'twill serve" all over
the front row's shoes. Faux blood. Real tears.
Twenty-five bucks a pop, going wage for stage death,
enough to spring for the twelve-hundredths carat ring,
its diminutive monument to bad acting—as even now
I wiggle too much to play a tree, head to shoulder
in blossom and bees. Tufts of pollen
dust my lips, thrumming as ours on closing night:
backseat stars adrift the Chevy's leather heaven.

Tomorrow

Never mind that. This time I'll not dawdle
in lawn chair beside the plum's yawn of bloom,
its white throat open and calling. I'll stop my ears
and shutter my eyes a field so narrow even sparrows
won't shadow the taxes you'd asked be done, just once,
on time. Somewhere between ambition and this tree
(who does not ask to blossom) squirms the dog
on short orbit, grassless half circle, his hapless
yapping charge collapsed in taut chain cough.
Somewhere between indolence and the worker bee
(who does not ask for rest) wings our late parakeet,
bird Houdini, who'd wriggle free to perch upon
a chair and call the tabby cat, *Tom, Tom, come here,*
till once he did. Somewhere between humility
and arrogance, the plum strums its wet tongue
in my ear, sure of fruit to come—as you were,
that hazy April of late days, when you brushed
the stick of gum across your flushed vulva,
then patiently rewrapped and mailed
this gift to me, so I might know as well.

Last Cut

Sunday's vase of   faded zinnia
trades cracked   glances with coreopsis
and asters arrayed   in tumbling arcs
as if to say what   disaster beauty forestalls
among the gaillardia   whose velvet flesh scents
my hands with pungence   I'll call fragrance
or stench, depending on   the hour, my beard's whiteness,
its length, the length of day   figured against this blush
of night, night's cheek against   the glass,
my glass half full but brimming   with shimmering light,
the light chained to a ceiling   I'd swear isn't there
because my head's rising so—   so too the leaves caught
before each touched down,   the down feather
freed from my tattered vest   and before that
from some goose chased   by fat Labradors
whose hinds looked crooked   as any dog's ought to be,
"to be" half of Prince Hamlet's   question but an answer
to all of mine, mine one face   among many upturned
as something lighter than   air sifts this September eve,
Eve in that garden no lovelier   than the dimpled honey bee,
drunken saint, lush with work   and pleasure
among the phlox' last flush,   plush as dusk caressing
the hive he'll not return to   to dance the honey jig
and tell his fellows where   the sweet's had down here,
here where not a soul stands   to turn us out
these adamantine gates   oh no, brother.

Gods of the Second Chance

I like the humble maker who'll suffice
with yardstick and upholstered plywood slats,
a little lever to lean the back back,
and *voila,* Mr. Shoemaker's got something
even he can't name. His Name-the-Chair contest
offers up *The Slack-Back, The Sit 'n Snooze,
The Comfort Carrier,* his winner blessing it
The La-Z-Boy, whence Bubba culture weds TV.
Add massage, built-in phone/modem/remote,
and who need leave its cushioned heaven?
Be thankful he wasn't Sir Thomas Crapper,
plumber-inventor whose throne we close
the door to mount in regal privacy,
his legacy the flush chain and clean gutters.

All this I've gleaned from one of those
sour millennial surveys of who invented what,
a book whose subject is less invention
than the author's envy of who did what
she didn't, and thus history's envy so often
involves knives, black sheep of problem solving.
The book blames Shoemaker for abetting
the beer belly, sloth, and Super Bowl spousal abuse,
though like any mortal a petulant god makes his goat,
he had limited options. Even a god can't undo
what another god does. What consolation
to be a goat, yes, but one graced to foretell
the future? Who, knowing what eventual evil
we'd wreak of it, would ever invent a thing?
What if Gutenberg could've imagined *Mein Kampf?*
What if Curie envisioned Teller's H-bomb?

Even Univac, balky but infallible,
couldn't compute the microchip or Internet porn.

Oh please. Stop the sniffing and pawing,
all the muzzled, puddled pleading.
We're the dog at our own basement door.
Come up into what scant light
February delivers. We, dear readers,
are not the first to thus screw up!
From fire, did Prometheus suspect napalm
and the cigarette? Amidst the millennial
lists we quaver over, let me praise my old Fender amp
and yellow Telecaster, to whose accompaniment
I wailed much best left unheard by dancers
and parents alike. Guitar whose feedback cloaked
my chimey rhyming of "moon" and "June"
with "Julie Calhoun." Amp whose blaring fare
did not spare my own ears, so now I nod
and smile at what my daughter pinches through
clinched teeth, hearing only a muffled sigh
of harmony coalesce paternal sense
I don't possess. Let's praise the eraser,
god of the second chance, without whom
Einstein's flawed formula might've cubed
our dark night's failure before he squared it.
Let's praise the delete key's beautiful impunity—
our knack for the right word held back,
the wrong keyed too freely. Let's praise
the blunt butter knife, ladder I offer
this beer-addled gnat to rise from my mug,
dry his wings in Einstein's light, then try again.

Confessional

I loved the ritual of spiritual spot removal.
I loved forgiveness, O cosmic delete key,
your dewy screw-ups zapped to ether
by fingering *Sorry* in a little holy water.
I loved the retrospective summary Father B
taught me: my sins spinning the twin Ferris wheel
venial and *mortal,* the latter reserved
for ax murder or presidential adultery.
I loved nods of mumbled prayer, their ransom.
None of that alone-in-your-room stuff for Rome.
Side by side you entered those booths,
the priest center-throned, wine-flushed.
Waiting on knee, you hoped for the daft one
who exacted small penance—say, three Hail Mary's,
the Our Father, a couple Glory Be's—
at least the young priest so you'll not shout
your mistakes like a carnie barking crowds
to this week's geek of earthly perdition.
Once I confessed the swoon of petting Julie,
who, kneeling in the next booth, burst out,
"You swore you'd never tell!" It was a sin
not to. Later, jaded by age, at the rat end
of my braided rope, I'd leave out things I'd done
or ladle in some I'd not, just to fluster Father B,
and then confess *that* lie—expurgation's high
sublime as sin. Such rush attends forgiveness,
as the priest knows of our bent-knee plea.
Thus my liturgical study, the bishop's workshops—
a way to wear black robes and still kiss girls.
I played dress-up to hear confession, morosely
curious as any rubbernecked accident gawker

slowing traffic in quest of mournful cry,
blood-spangled forehead. When finally I heard
what I'd thought I wanted, saw it full face and long
before the cops waved everyone move along,
we'd swapped places: I lay on the alluring gurney,
gory from the wreck of good intentions,
while victims motored away their lives. Wait.
That's what art would twist of it, dear gullible reader.
Nah, the usual dopey kid, I confess to dropping out
and stumbling home to punish the insolent green
of my parents' lawn. For this too I was forgiven.

Because I Wanted to Write a Happy Poem, I Thought of Harry Caray's Dying

No, not the actual instant, days delayed,
the cord unplugged, all the possible perils
of the possible soul—not that. I've in mind
his boozeless Valentine's dinner with Dutchie
the long-suffering, imperturbable wife.
His turning away the wine list with wrist flick
and head shake, lemon tottering his water
among ice. I've in mind beads his hand
stitched free raising that glass against
the stroke-stung tongue he'd wrap
around *Andres Gala-Rala-Allah-Angora,*
or *Hector Villa-Who-New-Wave-Ahh.*
Look, I'm no Cubs fan. I don't even have cable.
But Harry's "good friend" Pete Vonachen
my wife treats for diabetes, and I've driven
past Wainwright Welding in Moline whose picnic
Harry pronounced around Spike & Daisy's
50th announcement. All the malted hop
barhopping I'll not get into, or his feud
with Augie Busch the Teutonic Turtleneck.
Neither Bill Veeck nor Steve Stone's helmet head
Consort hair spray, nor the time Harry . . .
No, not that. Honestly, Harry's already
half out the door as I fondly remember him.
When he practiced death eleven years before
perfecting it, when he stroked and recuped
all spring, Harry beseeched Bill Murray to guest
play-by-play April 17, 1987. Good Friday.
And it was. My wife lay in labor, our first,

she undaunted but as shorn of good cheer
as the Easter lamb we'd planned the family dinner
over. She laughed and so contracted, afflicted
by a husband hyperventilating Lamaze
in her good ear until she hollered, sweetly,
how she couldn't hear a damn thing.
The ball game, Bill Murray. Then our daughter's
post postgame squall. When I think of Harry
it's of his masterful absence and my daughter's
entrance. He'd a lifetime of practiced exits—
closed-down bars, bottomless bottles. None as deft
as the toppled nod of acknowledgment he lent
that restaurant crowd, last he heard on earth: Applause.

Husk

It's testament to faith to say I'm not surprised
to find the kitchen luminous, granting
the fresh start forever eluding bad Godzilla,
who blubbers "What have I done?"
among the smoking rubble of Kyoto,
which, for once, this kitchen doesn't resemble
at 6:03 A.M., morning after a Super Bowl
party thrown as mere excuse to eat Mexican
and drink liqueur with little flecks of gold in it,
bought because my wife danced upon
our New Year's table after only two shots,
all black bra and sprung garters,
the table such an ocean it crashed
while salesmen stared in stunned amazement
and the band halted its cover of
Blood, Sweat, and Tears' "God Bless the Child,"
itself a bad cover of Billie Holiday's soulful original,
and it was my 42nd, after all,
three hundred drunks singing Happy Birthday,
so why shouldn't I be the one table dancing
with the woman in black bra and garters?

This started out seriously enough,
what with the mention of faith, but story
so sidetracked idea you end up with a box packed
with the rusty claw hammer and a carafe of burgundy,
a man trusting this marriage will last all the way
to the Rockies cabin—mine, I mean,
both the cheap wine *and* the cabin,
though I really mean the act of faith it takes
to pack hammer and carafe in cardboard,

how drinking one before using the other
may lead to all manner of breakage, which itself
can lead to rescue, as in BREAK GLASS IN CASE OF FIRE,
alarm clanging and you upon a burly shoulder
careening down a ladder as swiftly as I've invoked metaphor
to keep from being the religious poet
my friends fear I'll become, one who'll breathe into
an empty paper bag the booze came in
and ponder not his aching pagan head
but the soul within the husk of us this body is.

Beanstalk

How mundane those things that change us,
the line from crashed finch to sliced finger
to my daughter's loathing for homemade bread—
twelve tinny notes linking one story to another
as on "All Things Considered," where D.C.
cherry blossoms segue to Kabul's bone trade,
family plots unearthed because Pakistanis
will pay to grind the bones for cooking oil,
soap, chicken feed: the dead unplanted
to feed the starving and their starving poultry.
What's a body worth? Chickenfeed.
Yet, meaning *yes, but,* ask the dozen finches
who risk dusk for one last seed among
the husks brusquely tossed aside. Husk—a word
for those finch bodies as well as ours, though

what prize each enwraps is only speculation.
Chickenfeed? Being, Heidegger says, resides
in being-in-the-world not out of it. Yet.
How are we to know till we've left it,
smashed headlong into the glass we saw too late,
happy to be meeting the sister Other
eye to eye? Oh sure. I don't buy that.
Ask the crashed finch, flushed by the neighbor's
flabby tabby—tuft of feather on windowpane,
wing dust as serrated as our bread knife.
Worth what, a couple good rhymes.
Ask Jack in the Beanstalk, whose English bones
a giant threatened to grind for bread.
Ask Man Ray, fresh from Nazi Paris,
hitching NY to LA with a tie salesman

who pitched cheap wares at truck stop
and tourist trap. Paisley and polka dots,
collegiate hues, a blood red bold enough
to enliven even the stiffest pin stripe.
Capitalism's knot, the noose about our neck,
two for ten dollars. What can't be sold?
Safe in LA, Man Ray traded every tie he owned
for a shoe string he looped beneath his collar.
A price for everything, I'm thinking, as my daughter
slices her loaf of silence: "So hungry, they dig up
their dead?" At twelve, she's learned the names
of bone, muscle, organ, and the other names
for those other parts, too, in classroom
and all-night slumber party confession.
What's a body worth? *Fe, fi, fo, fum.*

Showering, she runs the well dry, pondering
the angle of water on belly and thigh.
The pump coughs air and still she stares,
unrecognizable, in the frantic antiseptic
bathroom light, mirror so fogged one body
meets the other along a path toward the river
she knows is there but can't see. Yet,
meaning *still to come.* The answer?
It turns out 98 cents, that old joke,
if hauled across the mountains to Pakistan.
Just 50 cents, 7,000 Afghanis, in Kabul.
Then what's a shovel for? To plant the dead
and dig them up. Meaning you shouldn't listen
to the radio if you've enough bread and few do.
What price guilt? Sliced finger and Band-Aid.

Fact is, each breath becomes bone
becomes dust. *Yes, but* what's a shovel for?
To plant the living who bloom right here.
Meaning if I had a hammer, if I had a hammer . . .
I'd still choose a shovel to plant the carload
of untagged, close-out perennials I bought

not knowing what, pledged to the double edge
of faith and desolation any life rides.
Any life, any ride. Who knows what you get?
Beans. I'd waited fall through summer to find out.
Ask Jack. I'd dusted bone meal so their roots
knuckled down. What can't be bought?
Go ask my daughter. It's time, time. *Yes, but.*
Oh shut up! I love this slew of blue lupine
and immaculate black-eyed Susan, a plenum of delphinium

blowing its gold-throated trumpet now. This now.

Illinois Poetry Series

Laurence Lieberman, Editor

History Is Your Own Heartbeat
Michael S. Harper (1971)

The Foreclosure
Richard Emil Braun (1972)

The Scrawny Sonnets and Other
Narratives
Robert Bagg (1973)

The Creation Frame
Phyllis Thompson (1973)

To All Appearances: Poems New and
Selected
Josephine Miles (1974)

The Black Hawk Songs
Michael Borich (1975)

Nightmare Begins Responsibility
Michael S. Harper (1975)

The Wichita Poems
Michael Van Walleghen (1975)

Images of Kin: New and Selected Poems
Michael S. Harper (1977)

Poems of the Two Worlds
Frederick Morgan (1977)

Cumberland Station
Dave Smith (1977)

Tracking
Virginia R. Terris (1977)

Riversongs
Michael Anania (1978)

On Earth as It Is
Dan Masterson (1978)

Coming to Terms
Josephine Miles (1979)

Death Mother and Other Poems
Frederick Morgan (1979)

Goshawk, Antelope
Dave Smith (1979)

Local Men
James Whitehead (1979)

Searching the Drowned Man
Sydney Lea (1980)

With Akhmatova at the Black Gates
Stephen Berg (1981)

Dream Flights
Dave Smith (1981)

More Trouble with the Obvious
Michael Van Walleghen (1981)

The American Book of the Dead
Jim Barnes (1982)

The Floating Candles
Sydney Lea (1982)

Northbook
Frederick Morgan (1982)

Collected Poems, 1930–83
Josephine Miles (1983; reissue, 1999)

The River Painter
Emily Grosholz (1984)

Healing Song for the Inner Ear
Michael S. Harper (1984)

The Passion of the Right-Angled Man
T. R. Hummer (1984)

Dear John, Dear Coltrane
Michael S. Harper (1985)

Poems from the Sangamon
John Knoepfle (1985)

In It
Stephen Berg (1986)

The Ghosts of Who We Were
Phyllis Thompson (1986)

Moon in a Mason Jar
Robert Wrigley (1986)

Lower-Class Heresy
T. R. Hummer (1987)

Poems: New and Selected
Frederick Morgan (1987)

Furnace Harbor: A Rhapsody of the
North Country
Philip D. Church (1988)

Bad Girl, with Hawk
Nance Van Winckel (1988)

Blue Tango
Michael Van Walleghen (1989)

Eden
Dennis Schmitz (1989)

Waiting for Poppa at the Smithtown
Diner
Peter Serchuk (1990)

Great Blue
Brendan Galvin (1990)

What My Father Believed
Robert Wrigley (1991)

Something Grazes Our Hair
S. J. Marks (1991)

Walking the Blind Dog
G. E. Murray (1992)

The Sawdust War
Jim Barnes (1992)

The God of Indeterminacy
Sandra McPherson (1993)

Off-Season at the Edge of the World
Debora Greger (1994)

Counting the Black Angels
Len Roberts (1994)

Oblivion
Stephen Berg (1995)

To Us, All Flowers Are Roses
Lorna Goodison (1995)

Honorable Amendments
Michael S. Harper (1995)

Points of Departure
Miller Williams (1995)

Dance Script with Electric Ballerina
Alice Fulton (reissue, 1996)

To the Bone: New and Selected Poems
Sydney Lea (1996)

Floating on Solitude
Dave Smith (3–volume reissue, 1996)

Bruised Paradise
Kevin Stein (1996)

Walt Whitman Bathing
David Wagoner (1996)

Rough Cut
Thomas Swiss (1997)

Paris
Jim Barnes (1997)

The Ways We Touch
Miller Williams (1997)

The Rooster Mask
Henry Hart (1998)

The Trouble-Making Finch
Len Roberts (1998)

Grazing
Ira Sadoff (1998)

Turn Thanks
Lorna Goodison (1999)

Traveling Light:
Collected and New Poems
David Wagoner (1999)

Some Jazz a While:
Collected Poems
Miller Williams (1999)

The Iron City
John Bensko (2000)

Songlines in Michaeltree:
New and Collected Poems
Michael S. Harper (2000)

Pursuit of a Wound
Sydney Lea (2000)

The Pebble: Old and New Poems
Mairi MacInnes (2000)

Chance Ransom
Kevin Stein (2000)

National Poetry Series

Eroding Witness
Nathaniel Mackey (1985)
Selected by Michael S. Harper

Palladium
Alice Fulton (1986)
Selected by Mark Strand

Cities in Motion
Sylvia Moss (1987)
Selected by Derek Walcott

The Hand of God and a Few
Bright Flowers
William Olsen (1988)
Selected by David Wagoner

The Great Bird of Love
Paul Zimmer (1989)
Selected by William Stafford

Stubborn
Roland Flint (1990)
Selected by Dave Smith

The Surface
Laura Mullen (1991)
Selected by C. K. Williams

The Dig
Lynn Emanuel (1992)
Selected by Gerald Stern

My Alexandria
Mark Doty (1993)
Selected by Philip Levine

The High Road to Taos
Martin Edmunds (1994)
Selected by Donald Hall

Theater of Animals
Samn Stockwell (1995)
Selected by Louise Glück

The Broken World
Marcus Cafagña (1996)
Selected by Yusef Komunyakaa

Nine Skies
A. V. Christie (1997)
Selected by Sandra McPherson

Lost Wax
Heather Ramsdell (1998)
Selected by James Tate

So Often the Pitcher Goes to Water until
It Breaks
Rigoberto González (1999)
Selected by Ai

Renunciation
Corey Marks (2000)
Selected by Philip Levine

Other Poetry Volumes

Local Men and *Domains*
James Whitehead (1987)

Her Soul beneath the Bone: Women's
Poetry on Breast Cancer
Edited by Leatrice Lifshitz (1988)

Days from a Dream Almanac
Dennis Tedlock (1990)

Working Classics: Poems on Industrial
Life
Edited by Peter Oresick and Nicholas Coles
(1990)

Hummers, Knucklers, and Slow Curves:
Contemporary Baseball Poems
Edited by Don Johnson (1991)

The Double Reckoning of Christopher
Columbus
Barbara Helfgott Hyett (1992)

Selected Poems
Jean Garrigue (1992)

New and Selected Poems, 1962–92
Laurence Lieberman (1993)

The Dig and *Hotel Fiesta*
Lynn Emanuel (1994)

For a Living: The Poetry of Work
Edited by Nicholas Coles and Peter Oresick
(1995)

The Tracks We Leave: Poems on
Endangered Wildlife of North America
Barbara Helfgott Hyett (1996)

Peasants Wake for Fellini's *Casanova* and
Other Poems
*Andrea Zanzotto; edited and translated by
John P. Welle and Ruth Feldman; drawings
by Federico Fellini and Augusto Murer*
(1997)

Moon in a Mason Jar and *What My Father
Believed*
Robert Wrigley (1997)

The Wild Card: Selected Poems, Early
and Late
*Karl Shapiro; edited by Stanley Kunitz and
David Ignatow* (1998)

Turtle, Swan and *Bethlehem in Broad
Daylight*
Mark Doty (2000)

Typeset in 10.5/13 Minion
with Gill Sans display
Designed by Dennis Roberts
Composed by Celia Shapland
for the University of Illinois Press
Manufactured by Thomson-Shore, Inc.

University of Illinois Press
1325 South Oak Street
Champaign, IL 61820-6903
www.press.uillinois.edu